Thomas Jefferson
The Third President

Carin T. Ford

Enslow Publishers, Inc.

40 Industrial Road	PO Box 38
Box 398	Aldershot
Berkeley Heights, NJ 07922	Hants GU12 6BP
USA	UK

http://www.enslow.com

Copyright © 2003 by Enslow Publishers, Inc.

Library of Congress Cataloging-in-Publication Data

Ford, Carin T.
    Thomas Jefferson : the third president / Carin T. Ford.
        v. cm. — (Heroes of American history)
    Contents: School days — Working hard — Voice for the colonies — Serving the people —
President Jefferson.
    ISBN 0-7660-1861-X (hardcover)
    1. Jefferson, Thomas, 1743–1826—Juvenile literature. 2. Presidents—United States—
Biography—Juvenile literature. [1. Jefferson, Thomas, 1743–1826. 2. Presidents.] I. Title.
II. Series.
    E332.79 .F67 2003
    973.4'6'092—dc21

                                                                2002010072

Printed in the United States of America

10 9 8 7 6 5 4 3 2 1

To Our Readers: We have done our best to make sure all Internet Addresses in this book were active and appropriate when we went to press. However, the author and the publisher have no control over and assume no liability for the material available on those Internet sites or on other Web sites they may link to. Any comments or suggestions can be sent by e-mail to comments@enslow.com or to the address on the back cover.

Illustration Credits: © Corel Corporation, p. 27; Enslow Publishers, Inc., pp. 12 (map), 25; Independence National Historical Park Collection. Portrait by Charles Willson Peale, p. 28; Library of Congress, pp. 3, 6, 7, 9(T), 9(B), 11, 12 (violin), 14, 15, 17, 19, 20, 22, 24, 26; National Archives, p. 21; White House Collection, courtesy White House Historical Association, p. 4; Wendie C. Old, p. 10.

Cover Credits: Library of Congress

Table of Contents

Thomas Jefferson

Chapter 1

School Days

When Thomas Jefferson was five years old, he went to a one-room schoolhouse. There he learned reading, writing, and arithmetic.

One afternoon, he got down on his knees behind the schoolhouse. Thomas prayed that it would soon be dinnertime. He was tired of school.

But Thomas would stay in school for many years. He would go on to college and become a lawyer, a musician, a scientist, an inventor, and a president.

Thomas was born April 13, 1743, to Peter and Jane Jefferson. He was the oldest boy of eight children. They lived at Shadwell, the family's farm in Virginia. At that time, Virginia was one of the thirteen American colonies ruled by England.

When Thomas was two, his family moved to a house on a tobacco plantation, a large farm. It was here that Thomas started going to school. He was a great reader. "I cannot live without books," he once wrote.

Thomas also learned many things outside school. His older sister Jane

This is one of the buildings on Shadwell farm.

taught him music. His father taught him about the plants and animals of the nearby forest. Thomas learned to hunt, fish, and ride a horse.

When Thomas was nine, his family moved back to their Shadwell home. Thomas was sent away to study with a teacher. He learned Greek, Latin, and French.

Thomas became a fine violinist. His mother liked to hear him play.

In 1757, Peter Jefferson died. Thomas was very sad without his father. He just wanted to be alone with his books and his music. Thomas was only fourteen years old, but he was now the head of the family.

Chapter 2

Working Hard

Not long after his father's death, Thomas traveled to a log schoolhouse about twelve miles from his home. He lived at the schoolhouse during the week. On the weekends, he went home.

Often, there was company at Shadwell, and that meant music and dancing. Thomas loved to play the violin. He practiced three hours a day.

In 1760, Thomas entered the College of William

and Mary in Williamsburg, Virginia. At sixteen, he was tall with red hair and freckles. He was a kind and friendly young man. He often went to parties, but he spent most of his time studying.

Thomas finished two years of college. After that he decided to become a lawyer. He spent his days reading law books and learning from George Wythe, who was a lawyer. Thomas listened to cases being tried in court and took notes on everything he heard and saw.

Thomas lived and studied in a small log schoolhouse like this one.

Here, in his friend George Wythe's office, Thomas studied law.

Thomas liked to keep track of everything. All his life, he wrote down how much money he spent, the books he read, and the vegetables he planted.

Thomas became a lawyer when he was twenty-four. He was very good at it, although he never really enjoyed being a lawyer.

He was more interested in politics. At age twenty-five, while also working as a lawyer, he was elected to the Virginia legislature. This was the lawmaking part of the state government.

Thomas wanted to make a law that would free the slaves. These were people who had been kidnapped in Africa and brought to America. They were bought and sold as property. On southern plantations, many slaves were forced to plant crops and pick cotton and tobacco. Others cooked and did housework. They were not paid for their work.

Thomas found that the other leaders in the Virginia legislature did not want to talk about slavery. They were more upset about the way

This poster tells of slaves for sale.

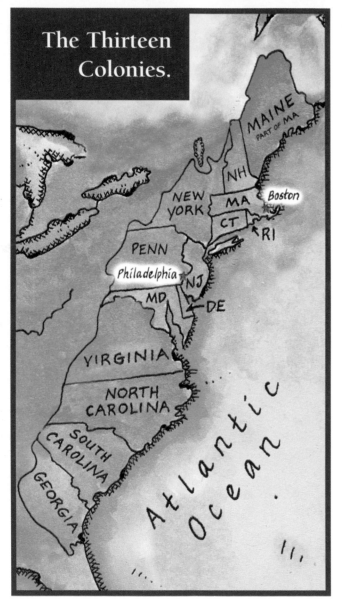

The Thirteen Colonies.

England was treating the American colonies. The government of England was placing taxes on items such as tea, glass, and paint.

The colonists had no say in the English government. They did not think they should have to follow laws made by a country so far away.

Thomas had other worries, too. In 1770, his family home—Shadwell—burned to the ground. The only thing that was not destroyed was his violin.

Chapter 3

Voice for
the Colonies

Although Shadwell had burned, Thomas soon had another place to live. He had been working for three years on a new home called Monticello, which means "little mountain" in Italian.

Thomas made the plan for the house himself. In colonial times, people built their homes on flat ground near the rivers and roads. But Thomas wanted his home to be on top of a mountain.

Tom loved fixing up his home and gardens at Monticello.

He wanted to look down on the hills and valleys.

In 1772, when Thomas was nearly thirty, he married Martha Wayles Skelton and brought her to live at Monticello. Martha loved music, so Thomas bought her a piano. Thomas often took out his violin, and the two played together. Over the years, they had six children. Only two of them, Martha and Mary, lived to be adults.

Thomas wanted to live quietly at Monticello, but the colonists needed his help. They were growing angrier with England every day. They did not like England's laws and taxes. What should they do?

Thomas had always been a very fine writer. Now he decided to write a paper complaining about how England was treating the American colonies.

Martha, below, and Thomas both loved music and books.

Leaders from the colonies came together for a meeting. It was called the First Continental Congress. Thomas could not attend, because he was sick. But his paper was read aloud.

When members of the English government found out about it, they did not like what Thomas had written. They called him a criminal.

The king of England sent soldiers to the colonies. They were ready to use guns to force the colonists to obey English laws. In April 1775, fighting broke out between the soldiers and the colonists.

The Second Continental Congress began in May 1775. Now the leaders of the colonies talked about becoming a free country. Thomas was asked to write another paper, which was named the Declaration of Independence.

The Declaration of Independence is one of the most important papers in our country's history. In it, Thomas wrote that all people have the right to be free and happy. He used strong but simple words to explain why Americans did not want to be ruled by England anymore.

On July 4, 1776, leaders of the colonies signed the Declaration of Independence. Americans were now fighting to win their freedom from England. This war, called the Revolutionary War, would last for eight years.

Thomas Jefferson, standing, shows the Declaration of Independence to Benjamin Franklin, left, and John Adams.

Chapter 4

Serving the People

In 1779, three years after the Declaration of Independence was signed, Thomas was elected Virginia's governor. The war against England was still going on.

English soldiers attacked many cities. But Virginia did not have enough soldiers or weapons. There was not enough money to buy food and guns. As governor, Thomas was blamed for Virginia's troubles.

At last the fighting ended, and it was time to talk

about peace. The Americans had won their freedom from England.

Thomas's term as governor was over. Now he could go back to working at Monticello. He also wrote a book about Virginia. It included the state's history, plant and animal life, geography, and laws.

In 1782, Thomas's wife died after being ill. He was so sad that he locked himself in his library and did not come out for three weeks. His daughter brought him food.

Thomas was governor of Virginia during the Revolutionary War.

Thomas, right, tried to make laws to end slavery.
Yet he still owned many slaves at Monticello.

But the country needed Thomas. He was elected
to Congress. There, he tried to make a law that would
not allow slavery in new states. His law did not pass.
Thomas also came up with a money system the whole

country could use. Before, each state had its own form of money. Thomas's plan called for pennies, dimes, and dollars.

When Thomas was forty-one, the United States government asked him to travel to Paris, France. John Adams and Benjamin Franklin were already there. The men talked to leaders from other countries. They made deals so America could trade goods with these countries.

Thomas stayed in France for five years. When he returned to America, George Washington had been elected the country's first president. He asked Thomas to work in the government and be the secretary of state. His job would be to help America get along with

Thomas said everyone should use dollars and cents. This is some Continental money.

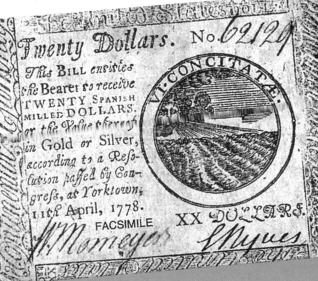

Thomas believed in the words he wrote: "All men are created equal."

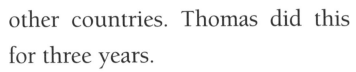

other countries. Thomas did this for three years.

In 1796, Thomas ran for president. John Adams won, and Thomas became the vice president.

Then, in 1801, Thomas was elected third president of the United States. He was fifty-seven years old. Thomas moved to Washington, D.C., the nation's new capital.

Thomas did not believe the president should be treated differently from anyone else. He wore plain clothes. At dinner, his guests sat at a round table. This way, no one would be at the head of the table and appear to be more important.

Thomas was president for eight years. Most Americans loved him.

Chapter 5

President Jefferson

Thomas was full of energy. He spent ten to thirteen hours each day at his desk, working on important papers for the government.

All his life, Thomas hated laziness. Every day he woke up at 5 A.M. to begin work. Later in the morning, he met with visitors. Then, Thomas always found time to exercise. He liked to go horseback riding every day.

Thomas was a very popular president.

Thomas held large dinners in the afternoon for as many as eighteen people. He offered new foods such as macaroni, and ice-cream balls wrapped in a warm crust. As part of his own diet, Thomas believed in eating a variety of vegetables.

By 6 P.M., Thomas expected his guests to leave. He had more work to do.

In 1803, Thomas had the United States buy some land from France. It stretched from the Mississippi River to the Rocky Mountains. With this land, called the Louisiana Territory, the United States was twice as big as before.

Ever since Thomas was a boy, he had been interested in plants and animals. Now he sent two men, Meriwether Lewis and William Clark, to explore the Louisiana Territory. They mapped out this huge area.

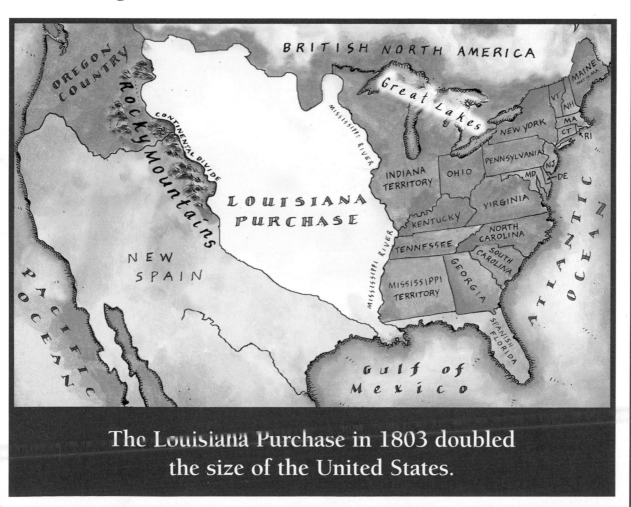

The Louisiana Purchase in 1803 doubled the size of the United States.

Lewis and Clark traveled thousands of miles. Sometimes the trip was very dangerous.

Because of Lewis and Clark's journey, many Americans wanted to move out west. They settled the land and built homes and farms there.

As president, Thomas lowered taxes and got rid of jobs he thought the government did not need. He set up a museum in the White House, with fossil bones from Kentucky and a new plow he had invented.

Thomas liked creating new things. He invented a chair that could spin around on its base, a closet with shelves that turned, and a bookstand that held five books open, so Thomas could read them all at once.

In 1809, Thomas's two terms as president were over. He returned to Monticello, where he spent much of his time fixing up his home and gardens.

When Thomas was seventy-six, he helped start a college, the University of Virginia. He designed the buildings himself. He even chose the teachers and decided what would be taught.

Thomas was always a simple man. He most enjoyed being alone with his books, his family, and a few old friends. He was always interested in learning and trying new ideas.

Thomas Jefferson was eighty-three years old when he died on July 4, 1826. It was exactly fifty years after the signing of the Declaration of Independence.

Thomas Jefferson always said that government should be fair to all people.

Timeline

1743~Born April 13 at Shadwell farm in Virginia.

1760~Enters the College of William and Mary, where he studies for two years.

1769~Becomes a member of the Virginia legislature.

1776~Writes the Declaration of Independence.

1779~Becomes governor of Virginia.

1790~Serves as secretary of state.

1797~Serves as vice president.

1801~Becomes president and serves for two terms.

1819~Helps start the University of Virginia.

1826~Dies on July 4 at his home, Monticello.

Words to Know

Congress—The chief group of lawmakers in the United States.

Declaration of Independence—The paper in which the American colonies state their freedom from England and become the United States of America.

First Continental Congress—A meeting of American leaders in 1774 to discuss the future of the colonies.

legislature—A group of people who make laws for a state or a country.

Revolutionary War—The war (1775–1783) in which the American colonies fought for freedom from England's rule.

Second Continental Congress—The second meeting of American leaders in 1775.

secretary of state—An adviser to the president who handles the United States' dealings with other countries.

Learn More

Books

Adler, David A. *A Picture Book of Thomas Jefferson*. New York: Holiday House, 1990.

Ferris, Jeri Chase. *Thomas Jefferson: Father of Liberty*. Minneapolis: Carolrhoda Books, Inc., 1998.

Giblin, James Cross. *Thomas Jefferson: A Picture Book Biography*. New York: Scholastic, 1994.

Internet Addresses

Short biographies of Thomas Jefferson, with links to other information.
  <http://www.monticello.org/resources/people/biography.html>

  <http://www.ipl.org/div/potus/tjefferson.html>

  <http://www.americastory.gov/cgi-bin/page.cgi/aa/jefferson>

Index